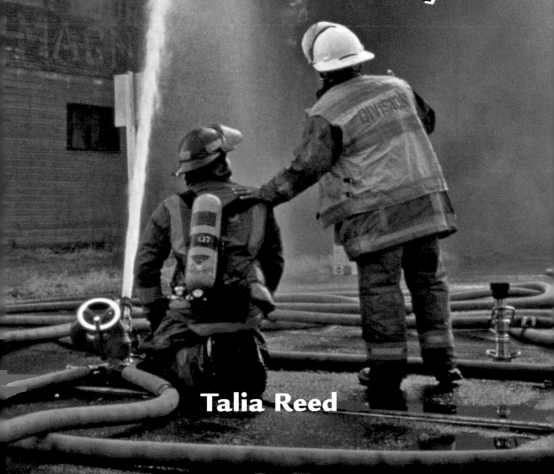

NATIONAL
GEOGRAPHIC

Serving the Community

Talia Reed

Contents

Strong Communities 3

Safety. 4

Roads 6

Cleaning and Repairing 8

Parks 10

Learning. 12

Community Leaders 14

What Can You Do? 16

Strong Communities

The United States is made of many communities, large, small, and in-between. Cities, towns, and villages are all different kinds of communities.

Communities need people. They need workers who provide services. They need good citizens. They also need leaders. Together, all of these people serve their communities. They help to make them strong.

Safety

Many people in a community work to keep others safe. Some people work as crossing guards near schools. They make sure school children are safe in traffic.

Firefighters help prevent fires and put out fires when they happen. Police officers make sure people obey laws. They also help in emergencies.

Kids Can Help

This girl and her father use the traffic signal to cross the street safely.

Roads

Some people who work for our community help to keep the roads safe. They fix potholes and cracks. They clean the streets, and in winter they might need to plow snow. It's a big job to keep roads safe and clean. Sometimes roadwork even needs to be done in the middle of the night.

This man uses a snow blower to clear snow.

Kids Can Help

This boy is shoveling snow outside his home. This helps keep the sidewalk safe for everyone in his community.

7

Cleaning and Repairing

Some community workers keep the community clean. They collect trash. They also collect paper, glass, metal, plastic, and other materials to be recycled.

Other workers take care of things that belong to the community. They repair things that are broken, such as water pipes or streetlight bulbs. Painting community buildings is another way that workers take care of the community.

Kids Can Help

These children are
working together
to pick up litter.

9

Parks

Some people who work for the community help take care of public parks and gardens. They plant and take care of flowers, trees, and lawns. Sometimes they help organize special community events that take place in parks or other public spaces.

These people are enjoying an art fair in a park.

Kids Can Help

These children are planting bushes as part of a community project.

Learning

Some people who work in communities help others learn. They work in school classrooms, lunchrooms, and offices. They work in libraries and museums. These people help make communities interesting places to live.

Communities provide schools so that all children can learn.

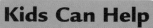

Kids Can Help

This boy is returning his library books on time. Now others can check them out, too.

Community Leaders

All communities have leaders. Some cities and towns have a mayor. Some also have a city council. Citizens vote for community leaders in an election.

The mayor and the city council work together. They make important decisions about the community.

These citizens are voting to elect the leaders of their community.

The mayor of a community sometimes gives speeches at special events.

Kids Can Help

This girl has made a poster. It tells community leaders and others how she feels about her school.

What Can You Do?

Communites need leaders, workers, and good citizens. Good citizens care about what happens in their communities. They work to take care of their communities.

What do you already do to help your community? What else can you do?